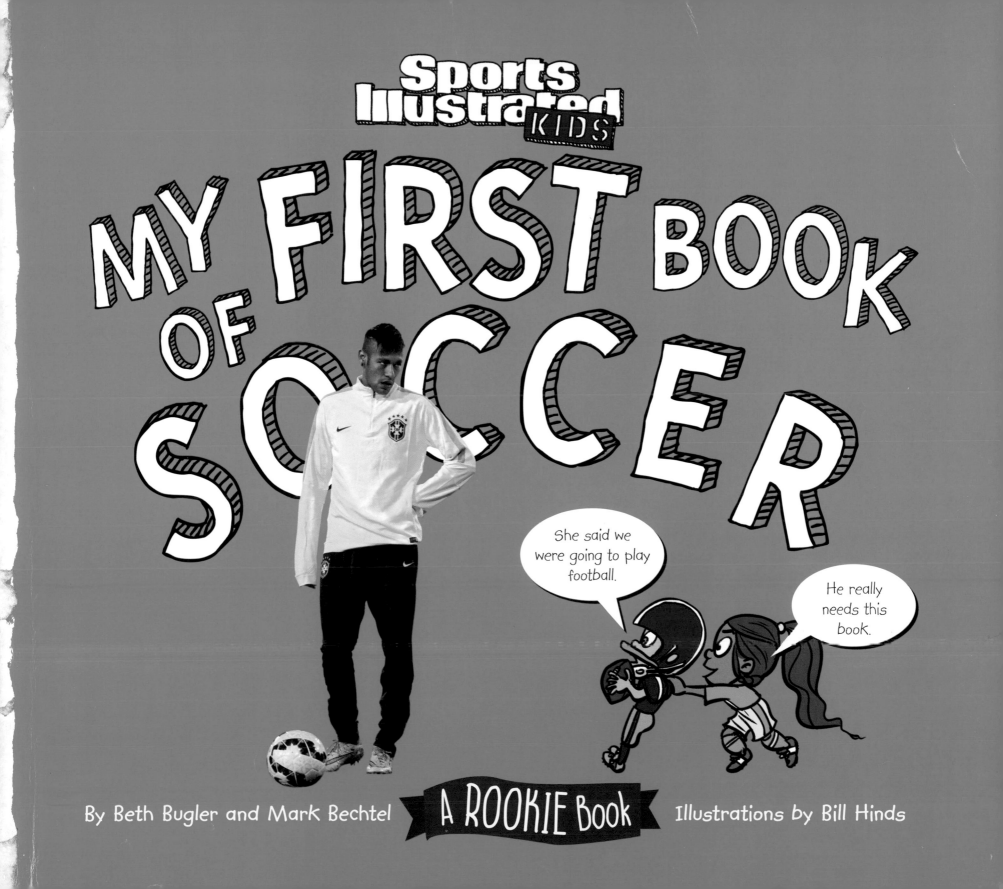

Soccer, or football as it's known in the rest of the world, is a sport played by

TWO TEAMS.

The players try to score goals by getting a ball into a net without using their hands. Each team has

11 PLAYERS

on the field at one time.

I think my face is frozen.

Can we use our hands for the photo?

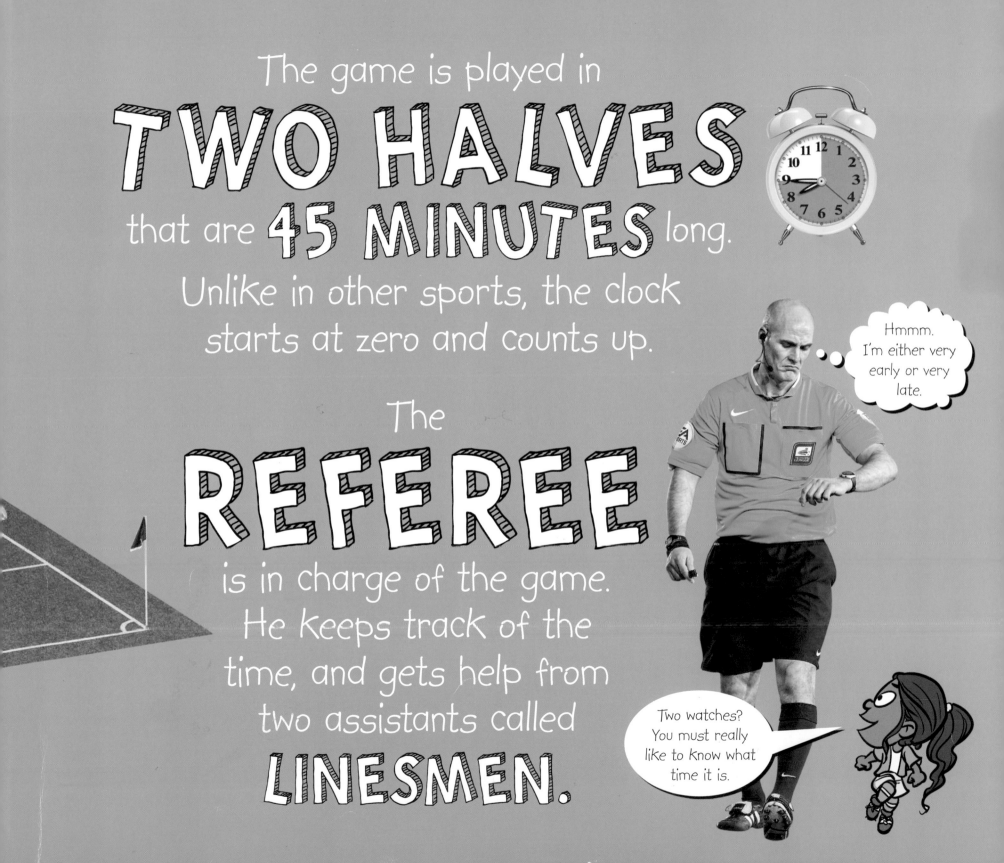

The players line up at different positions.

Hey guys, which is the position that runs the least?

Dude, where's that five bucks you owe me?

FORWARDS try to score goals.

DEFENDERS try to keep the other team from scoring.

MIDFIELDERS try to help score goals AND help keep the other team from scoring.

The GOALKEEPER

is the only player who can use his hands. His job is to keep the ball from going into the goal. He wears gloves and a different color jersey.

I will not let you down!

So are you the only one I can high-five?

PEEEEEEEP!

The referee blows his whistle, and the game starts with a

KICKOFF!

The team with the ball is the
ATTACKING
team.

The other players are the
DEFENDING
team.

She's got the ball and makes a  **PASS** to her teammate

Look out!
Here comes a defender
who makes a

TACKLE

and steals away the
ball with his foot.

Maybe this will
come in handy
after all.

Whoops. A player knocked the ball over the sideline. The other team gets to take a

THROW-IN

from the spot where the ball went out of play.

Hey, Justin! I'm open!

BMO

33

She's got the goal in sight and takes a

SHOT.

It's headed toward the net. Will the goalkeeper stop it?

TIME
21:10

But the ball went over the goal line. Since the defending team was the last to touch it, the other team gets a

CORNER KICK

from the nearest corner flag.

TIME
39:16

The kick comes in high, so his teammate jumps up and hits a

HEADER

toward the net.

That's how the pros use their heads!

The game gets ready to start again. But first, the coach decides to make a

SUBSTITUTION.

A new player comes off the bench and into the game.

Does she have to go home now?

The linesman has his flag up because number 8 was

OFFSIDE.

That means he was closer to the goal than all of the defensive players when he got the ball. The rule prevents players from just hanging out near the net and scoring easy goals.

Is that a quarter in the grass?

Ah! There goes my plan to score!

Look! She tries to make a tackle, but she trips her opponent instead. That's a

FOUL!

Even I know tripping is wrong!

Since the foul was serious, the referee shows the player a

YELLOW CARD.

That's a warning that he'd better not do it again.

The attacking team gets a

FREE KICK.

YELLOW CARD.
YELLOW CARD.
YELLOW CARD.

Stop . . .
STOP!

The attacking team gets to place the ball where the foul happened. They can either pass the ball or take a shot at the goal. The defense sets up a

WALL.

But it looks like he's going to try to bend the ball around them and into the net!

No way I'm sitting on THAT wall.

TIME
57:01

Oh, no! A player who already has a yellow card has committed another bad foul. The referee brings out a

RED CARD

and sends him out of the game.

The ball has gone over the goal line, but this time it was kicked out by the attacking team. That means the other side's goalie gets to take a

GOAL KICK.

She places the ball on the goal box and knocks it all the way down the field.

The clock has almost reached 90 minutes, and the score is tied. Whoa! Did you see that? That defender knocked down the ball with his hand! The ref calls a

HAND BALL.

And since it happened in the penalty area, the other team gets a . . .

...PENALTY KICK.

They get a free shot and only the goalkeeper is allowed to try to stop it.

It goes in! Her team has the lead!

Writers: Beth Bugler, Mark Bechtel
Designer: Beth Bugler
Illustrator: Bill Hinds
Production Manager: Hillary Leary

Copyright © 2017 Time Inc. Books

Published by Liberty Street, an imprint of
Time Inc. Books
225 Liberty Street
New York, NY 10281

ISBN: 978-1-68330-002-1
Library of Congress Control Number:
2016958271

First edition, 2017
1 TLF 17
10 9 8 7 6 5 4 3 2 1

We welcome your comments and suggestions
about Time Inc. Books.

Time Inc. Books
Attention: Book Editors
P.O. Box 62310
Tampa, FL 33662-2310
(800) 765-6400

timeincbooks.com

Time Inc. Books products may be purchased
for business or promotional use. For
information on bulk purchases, please
contact Christi Crowley in the Special Sales
Department at (845) 895-9858.